for Men

A LIFE TO GIVE

Readings and Scripture
for the Heart of a Man

for Men

A
Life to
Give

Readings and Scripture
for the Heart of a Man

A LIFE TO GIVE:
Readings and Scriptures for the Heart of a Man

Printed in the United States of America
ISBN 0-8054-3150-0

To order additional copies of this book,
call 1-800-448-8032.

1 2 3 4 07 06 05 04

CONTENTS

INTRODUCTION

Maybe books are not your thing. Or maybe you typically go in for reading that's much more substantial and heavy.

But we're praying that this little book will find a place in your life, because the subjects which are talked about inside are ones you very likely face at least once in an average week—and probably much more often than that.

And, not at all surprisingly, each of the life issues addressed in here are scoured and covered in the pages of the Bible—a book many people find to be exclusively other-worldly, but which continues to remain as current as the afternoon mail, generation after generation.

So come in for a while and come back when you can. These are Scripture verses every man needs to have as close as his hip pocket, as well as ideas and insights that have the power to pick us up and take us a little higher.

We've been praying you'd be here. And we hope God blesses your stay.

STRESS

God is our refuge and strength, a helper who is always found in times of trouble. Therefore we will not be afraid, though the earth trembles and the mountains topple into the depths of the seas, though its waters roar and foam and the mountains quake with its turmoil.

Psalm 46:1-3

A BREAK IN THE ACTION

There was a day not too many years ago when the futurists and trend watchers were reporting that we were coming into our glory years. With the wide-scale emergence of the personal computer and the simpler life we'd enjoy from today's modern conveniences, ours was to be the generation of the shorter work week, the calmer pace, the boundless, measureless life. Our biggest challenge was supposed to be choosing how to spend all this extra time we'd have on our hands.

Very funny.

Because what the forecasters forgot to consider was that they were dealing not just with science and technology but with people—people with human natures— people who weren't content that a package which used to take three days to be delivered could now arrive in two. Surely it could be done overnight. And so, the speed of life became no match for the speed of our expectations. The evening newspaper became a useless rag of stories we'd already seen on the Web or heard on the radio. The video game system that used to be updated every six years was now old-hat after six months. Cell phones which were once reserved for roadside emergencies were now being used to order pizzas and whatever else you can do with three thousand free minutes a weekend. (Are there even three thousand minutes *in a weekend?*)

Yep, we are now available by pager, voice mail, and GPS coordinates every minute of every day. We are constantly competing with rival companies who have no problem chewing up and spitting out human resources, if that's the cost of doing things quicker and cheaper. Our home life, our family life, the dream we had of ever just sitting down with a cup of coffee and thinking about absolutely nothing for a half hour is nearly gone.

Lord, help us.

Well, God's Word is help. It doesn't mow the grass or take out the trash for us, but it does provide a framework for living through a period of life when leaner and meaner seem to be our only options.

Through the pages of the Bible, God offers us perspective. He teaches us that all our days were "written in [His] book and planned before a single one of them began" (Psalm 139:16). He gives us an eternal outlook that makes today's urgencies seem a little less traumatic . . . and eternity's rewards a little sweeter to think about.

He offers us strength—strength that is somehow "perfected in weakness" (2 Corinthians 12:9). On a routine, orderly day, we may feel like we can make it just fine without God and His Word, but crank the chaos meter to a certain level, and we realize our strength is not coming from us.

He also offers us peace—peace "which surpasses every thought" (Philippians 4:7)—peace that shows up right when we need it . . . if we're willing to rest in it, embrace it, and receive it.

Yes, our lives may be one big stress-maker after another. But our God is the one big Rock that makes even the most daily or deadly challenge seem wimpy by comparison.

Trouble and distress terrify him: they over-
power him like a king poised for battle.

Job 15:24

Show us favor, LORD, show us favor,
for we've had more than enough contempt.

Psalm 123:3

God, hear my cry;
pay attention to my prayer.
I call to You from the ends of the earth
when my heart is without strength.
Lead me to a rock that is high above me,
for You have been a refuge for me,
a strong tower in the face of the enemy.
I will live in Your tent forever,
take refuge under the shelter of Your wings....
Then I will continually sing of Your name,
fulfilling my vows day by day.

Psalm 61:1-4, 8

This is the day the LORD has made;
let us rejoice and be glad in it.
LORD, save us! LORD, please grant us success!

Psalm 118:24-25

Surely this is my suffering, and I must bear it.

Jeremiah 10:19b

For consider Him who endured such hostility from sinners against Himself, so that you won't grow weary and lose heart.

Hebrews 12:3

Stop your fighting—and know that I am God,
exalted among the nations,
exalted on the earth.

Psalm 46:10

He saw [the disciples] being battered as they rowed, because the wind was against them.

Around three in the morning He came toward them walking on the sea, and wanted to pass by them. When they saw Him walking on the sea, they thought it was a ghost and cried out; for they all saw Him and were terrified.

Immediately He spoke with them and said, "Have courage! It is I. Don't be afraid." Then He got into the boat with them, and the wind ceased.

Mark 6:48-51

Peace I leave with you. My peace I give to you. I do not give to you as the world gives. Your heart must not be troubled or fearful.

John 14:27

For the waywardness
   of the inexperienced will kill them,
   and the complacency of fools
   will destroy them.
But whoever listens to me will live securely
   and be free from the fear of danger.

Proverbs 1:32-33

The Bible is the one book to which any thoughtful man may go with any honest question of life or destiny and find the answer of God by honest searching.

—John Ruskin

7

For as the sufferings of Christ overflow to us, so our comfort overflows through Christ. If we are afflicted, it is for your comfort and salvation; if we are comforted, it is for your comfort, which is experienced in the endurance of the same sufferings that we suffer. . . .

For we don't want you to be unaware, brothers, of our affliction that took place in the province of Asia: we were completely overwhelmed—beyond our strength—so that we even despaired of life. However, we personally had a death sentence within ourselves so that we would not trust in ourselves, but in God who raises the dead.

He has delivered us from such a terrible death, and He will deliver us; we have placed our hope in Him that He will deliver us again.

2 Corinthians 1:5-6, 8-10

Therefore don't worry about tomorrow, because tomorrow will worry about itself. Each day has enough trouble of its own.

Matthew 6:34

But as for you, keep a clear head about everything, endure hardship, do the work of an evangelist, fulfill your ministry.

2 Timothy 4:5

Share in suffering as a good soldier of Christ.

2 Timothy 2:3

Strengthen your tired hands and weakened knees, and make straight paths for your feet, so that what is lame may not be dislocated, but healed instead.

Hebrews 12:12-13

Say to the faint-hearted: "Be strong; do not fear!"

Isaiah 35:4a

DISCIPLINE

Make every effort to supplement your faith with goodness, goodness with knowledge, knowledge with self-control, self-control with endurance, endurance with godliness, godliness with brotherly affection, and brotherly affection with love.

2 Peter 1:5-7

DAY IN, DAY OUT

Discipline is not something we either have or we don't have. It's something we're either gaining or we're losing. Like all character traits, discipline is either in the process of being strengthened and reinforced in our lives each day, or it's being weakened and compromised.

That's why the verses from 2 Peter on the previous page are so important. They detail a progression of growth, showing us that the work of each day is simply to add a few, small layers of structure onto our character base. We certainly don't just wake up one morning with knowledge and self-control waiting for us in the living room, ready to take us from zero to seventy in 6.9 seconds. Instead it's like the growth we see (but don't see) in our kids each day. People who haven't been around them for a year or two can hardly believe how much they've grown, yet *we* can pretty much only see it when we're looking at old home movies.

That's the way character works.

And discipline is how it gets done.

We're familiar with coaches and players fielding questions from reporters, insisting that their team is approaching the rest of the season "one game at a time." And even though this canned cliché has worn out most of its meaning, even though it sails predictably past our ears without saying anything new, the idea behind it remains as true as it is uneventful.

We take life one day at a time. And when the dust has cleared, we've either moved the ball ahead or been thrown for a loss. There is no such day as a no-gainer.

Until we can see this *momentum* aspect of discipline, until we realize that it's a drive not a destination, until we can be content with putting one or two bricks of it in place consistently over time, we'll continue to find ourselves living undisciplined lives. Yeah, we'll show it in spurts, we'll feel it at times, but we won't enjoy its steady walk into strength and dependability.

But the good news is this: no rule says you have to punt on fourth down. Even if developing discipline has been a problem for you, you're just one nice play away from getting a fresh, new start. The victory won't be won just because you moved the chains this time. You'll still have to line up again . . . and block and hit and run and execute. But you'll look up one day with a whole lot of positive yardage under your belt. And you'll never want to go back to fourth and long again.

Maybe your discipline needs to start where you are right now—with spending time with God in prayer and in his Word.

Maybe it involves making deliberate choices with your time and your calendar, getting in the habit of doing one thing on your top priority list day in and day out.

But it can happen. You can do it. Then you'll start enjoying a disciplined life . . . and a whole bunch of other new characters.

Patience is better than power,
and controlling one's temper,
than capturing a city.

Proverbs 16:32

For when we were in the flesh, the sinful passions operated through the law in every part of us and bore fruit for death.

But now we have been released from the law, since we have died to what held us, so that we may serve in the new way of the Spirit and not in the old letter of the law.

Romans 7:5-6

Therefore, get your minds ready for action, being self-disciplined, and set your hope completely on the grace to be brought to you at the revelation of Jesus Christ.

As obedient children, do not be conformed to the desires of your former ignorance but, as the One who called you is holy, you also are to be holy in all your conduct; for it is written, "Be holy, because I am holy."

1 Peter 1:13-16

15

LORD, You are our Father;
  we are the clay, and You are our potter;
  we all are the work of Your hand.

Isaiah 64:8

Christ has liberated us into freedom.
Therefore stand firm and don't submit again to
a yoke of slavery.

Galatians 5:1

I will instruct you and show you the way to go;
  with My eye on you, I will give counsel.
Do not be like a horse or mule,
  without understanding,
    that must be controlled with bit and bridle,
    or else it will not come near you.
Many pains come to the wicked,
  but the one who trusts in the LORD
  will have faithful love surrounding him.

Psalm 32:8-10

I love those who love me,
  and those who search for me find me.

Proverbs 8:17

So then, brothers, we are not obligated to the flesh to live according to the flesh, for if you live according to the flesh, you are going to die. But if by the Spirit you put to death the deeds of the body, you will live.

Romans 8:12-13

But endurance must do its complete work, so that you may be mature and complete, lacking nothing.

James 1:4

Scholars may quote Plato in their studies, but the hearts of millions will quote the Bible at their daily toil, and draw strength from its inspiration, as the meadows draw it from the brook.

—M. Daniel Conway

Endure it as discipline: God is dealing with you as sons. For what son is there whom a father does not discipline? But if you are without discipline—which all receive—then you are illegitimate children and not sons.

Furthermore, we had natural fathers discipline us, and we respected them. Shouldn't we submit even more to the Father of spirits and live?

For they disciplined us for a short time based on what seemed good to them, but He does it for our benefit, so that we can share His holiness.

No discipline seems enjoyable at the time, but painful. Later on, however, it yields the fruit of peace and righteousness to those who have been trained by it.

Hebrews 12:7-11

If anyone wants to come with Me, he must deny himself, take up his cross daily, and follow Me. For whoever wants to save his life will lose it, but whoever loses his life because of Me will save it. What is a man benefited if he gains the whole world, yet loses or forfeits himself?

Luke 9:23-25

But the fruit of the Spirit is love, joy, peace, patience, kindness, goodness, faith, gentleness, self-control. Against such things there is no law.

Now those who belong to Christ Jesus have crucified the flesh with its passions and desires. If we live by the Spirit, we must also follow the Spirit.

Galatians 5:22-25

Be sober! Be on the alert! Your adversary the Devil is prowling around like a roaring lion, looking for anyone he can devour.

Resist him, firm in the faith, knowing that the same sufferings are being experienced by your brothers in the world.

1 Peter 5:8-9

BALANCE

You are to labor six days and do all your work, but the seventh day is a Sabbath to the LORD your God. . . . For the LORD made the heavens and the earth, the sea, and everything in them in six days; then He rested on the seventh day. Therefore the LORD blessed the Sabbath day and declared it holy.

Exodus 20:9-10a, 11

ALL
WORK,
NO PLAY?

It's a lot easier to ask the questions than it is to give the answers. Questions like . . .

• What should I do when the end of the day gets here, and I don't have it all done?

• How can I tell my boss I don't have time for this . . . without setting myself up to be replaced?

• My salary just isn't enough. Isn't there some way I can earn some extra money?

• When am I ever going to have time to do the things I need to do around the house?

• How many more of my kids' activities am I going to have to miss before I make some changes around here?

• What is keeping me from getting more done? Am I wasting time on the wrong things?

Sure enough, these are tough days for a guy seeking balance. Just about every company in America is trying to do more with less. Therefore, just about all of us are finding a lot less of ourselves to go around.

So there are no easy answers. And everyone's situation is a little different.

But does God have anything to say about what to do with work that's out of balance?

The Bible's sum wrap-up seems to be this: "Nothing is better for man than to eat, drink, and let himself experience good times in his struggle. I see that even this is from the hand of God" (Ecclesiastes 2:24).

So the Bible admits to struggle. I mean, we brought this on ourselves. Adam was created to work and to tend the garden—there's nothing cursed about that. It was a job designed to give him gratifying fulfillment and usefulness. But when he sinned, God added to work its "struggle" component as a punishment and a reminder of how much we need him. So not every day has a spring in its step. Not every morning is like that first spring Saturday when we fire up the mower and wonder why this becomes such a chore by around June and August.

Struggle is common to all of us. We may as well get used to that.

But the Bible does promise us "good times" in the midst of struggle. Not everyone will recognize these "good times" when they see them. Maybe you've had a hard time spotting them yourself lately. But God loves bringing "good" out of things that seem not-so-good.

So if we'll work on having hearts that are bursting at the seams to please Him, He'll show us where the high spots are in our most hectic day.

If our love for our family is so deep that they know we want to be with them and enjoy them, we'll be able to go to the games and practices we need to, and they'll understand when we honest-to-goodness can't.

If our spirits are totally submitted to obeying God and seeking His will through every day's work, He'll keep us focused on the most important things even while we're doing the necessary things.

Life may not balance out every day. But taken as a total, our lives can become sane and reasonable.

And it'll be God's work and God's work alone when it happens.

Do not lack diligence; be fervent in spirit; serve the Lord.

Romans 12:11

Now we command and exhort such people, by the Lord Jesus Christ, that quietly working, they may eat their own bread. Brothers, do not grow weary in doing good.

2 Thessalonians 3:12-13

But we encourage you, brothers, to do so even more, to seek to lead a quiet life, to mind your own business, and to work with your own hands, as we commanded you, so that you may walk properly in the presence of outsiders and not be dependent on anyone.

1 Thessalonians 4:10b-12

And whatever you do, in word or in deed, do everything in the name of the Lord Jesus, giving thanks to God the Father through Him.

Colossians 3:17

What profit does the worker gain when he struggles? I see the business that God gives people to keep them busy. He has arranged everything appropriately in its time and has also put forever in their hearts. Still no one can discover the accomplishment God has accomplished from beginning to end.

I know nothing is better for anyone than to rejoice and to accomplish good with their lives. Also, it is God's gift whenever anyone eats, drinks, and experiences good in all his struggle.

Ecclesiastes 3:9-13

Therefore, whether you eat or drink, or whatever you do, do everything for God's glory.

1 Corinthians 10:31

You are to conduct yourselves in reverence during this time of temporary residence. For you know that you were redeemed from your empty way of life inherited from the fathers, not with perishable things, like silver or gold, but with the precious blood of Christ.

1 Peter 1:17b-19a

Now the end of all things is near; therefore, be clear-headed and disciplined for prayer. . . . Based on the gift they have received, everyone should use it to serve others, as good managers of the varied grace of God. If anyone speaks, his speech should be like the oracles of God; if anyone serves, his service should be from the strength God provides, so that in everything God may be glorified through Jesus Christ. To Him belong the glory and the power forever.

1 Peter 4:7, 10-11

The Bible goes equally to the cottage of the peasant and the palace of the king. It enters men's closets, directs their conduct, and mingles in all the grief and cheerfulness of life.

—Theodore Parker

Everything has its appointed hour,
every matter its time under the heavens:
a time to give birth and a time to die;
a time to plant
and a time to uproot what is planted;
a time to kill and a time to heal;
a time to tear down and a time to build up;
a time to weep and a time to laugh;
a time to mourn and a time to dance;
a time to throw stones away
and a time to gather stones;
a time to embrace and a time
to keep one's distance from embracing;
a time to search and a time to count as lost;
a time to keep and a time to throw away;
a time to tear and a time to sew;
a time to be silent and a time to speak;
a time to love and a time to hate;
a time for war and a time for peace.

Ecclesiastes 3:1-8

Be in agreement with one another. Do not be proud; instead, associate with the humble. Do not be wise in your own estimation. Do not repay anyone evil for evil. Try to do what is honorable in everyone's eyes. If possible, on your part, live at peace with everyone.

Romans 12:16-18

For if anyone considers himself to be something when he is nothing, he is deceiving himself. But each person should examine his own work, and then he will have a reason for boasting in himself alone, and not in respect to someone else. For each person will have to carry his own load.

Galatians 6:3-5

If anyone thinks he is religious, without controlling his tongue but deceiving his heart, his religion is useless. Pure and undefiled religion before our God and Father is this: to look after orphans and widows in their distress and to keep oneself unstained by the world.

James 1:26-27

DECISIONS

Now if any of you lacks wisdom, he should ask God, who gives to all generously and without criticizing, and it will be given to him. But let him ask in faith without doubting. For the doubter is like the surging sea, driven and tossed by the wind. That person should not expect to receive anything from the Lord.

James 1:5-7

THIS WAY, THAT WAY

Among the decisions that are the hardest to make are the ones we have to make in a pinch—decisions where seconds count, where every minute of delay shrinks both our options and our margin for error. There are also certain environments we find ourselves in (or *place* ourselves in) where making good choices is more difficult than usual—when we feel tired and beat up from a long ordeal of some kind, when our patience is thin or our defenses are down.

There are choices between friends and family, between safe and chancy, between good and better . . . or the even more harrowing choice: between bad and worse—when neither decision has an upside, only a slightly less painful one.

I'm sure most of the good how-to books on the shelves are just full of sound advice and strategy tips for taking the edge off of these tough spots in life. A good many of their ideas are probably worth reading and applying where we can.

But God's Word, though never a proponent of being lazy or unprepared, leaves us with an idea that sends icy chills down our backs, especially those of us who like to reduce danger to a minimum, who feel better when we've had time to carefully examine all the factors that could come into play, who are more comfortable having all the lines filled in and the diagrams drawn.

God's command?

"Trust me."

Ooo. At once we're speechless and yet not totally convinced. We're sure there's a better way, a more practical solution, a few notebooks of research available to give us more concrete direction, and yet . . . no better plan of action comes to mind.

And so we trust him—for wisdom (like in James 1:5), for guidance (Proverbs 3:5), for discernment (Romans 12:2), for counsel (Isaiah 11:2), for the knowledge of his will and desire (Ephesians 5:17).

Something about it still seems shaky. We wonder whether he knows what he's talking about. Yet when it's all said and done—no matter how many thoughts and worries and one-man conversations we've had with ourselves—do we have anything more solid to stand on than his Word and his wisdom?

No. We just have him. And he's enough.

Now, that doesn't mean most decisions will be easy. It doesn't mean they'll even look like the correct ones right away. This side of heaven, in fact, we may never fully grasp all the reasons God had for leading us this certain way.

And yet in the loving fatherhood of God, even our missteps and mistaken judgments can be rescued from the brink of disaster . . . and redirected toward his higher purposes and another chance to trust him more fully.

So in reality, the safest place to make a decision is in the one place we may feel the most vulnerable and exposed—in full submission to God and his will.

It's the best decision we'll make all day.

Brothers, don't be childish in your thinking, but be infants in evil and adult in your thinking.

1 Corinthians 14:20

Trust in the LORD with all your heart,
  and do not rely on your own understanding;
  think about Him in all your ways,
  and He will guide you on the right paths.
Don't consider yourself to be wise;
  fear the LORD and turn away from evil.

Proverbs 3:5-7

Pay careful attention, then, to how you walk— not as unwise people but as wise— making the most of the time, because the days are evil. So don't be foolish, but understand what the Lord's will is.

Ephesians 5:15-17

Do not be conformed to this age, but be transformed by the renewing of your mind, so that you may discern what is the good, pleasing, and perfect will of God.

Romans 12:2

You teach me wisdom deep within.

Psalm 51:6b

But be doers of the word and not hearers only, deceiving yourselves. Because if anyone is a hearer of the word and not a doer, he is like a man looking at his own face in a mirror; for he looks at himself, goes away, and right away forgets what kind of man he was.

But the one who looks intently into the perfect law of freedom and perseveres in it, and is not a forgetful hearer but a doer who acts—this person will be blessed in what he does.

James 1:22-25

The Spirit of the LORD will rest on Him—
a Spirit of wisdom and understanding,
a Spirit of counsel and strength, a Spirit
of knowledge and of the fear of the LORD.

Isaiah 11:2

Then you will understand righteousness,
justice, and integrity—every good path.

Proverbs 2:9

For wisdom will enter your heart,
  and knowledge will delight your soul.
Discretion will watch over you,
  and understanding will guard you.

Proverbs 2:10-11

Wisdom is better than weapons of war.

Ecclesiastes 9:18a

*The real influence of the Bible cannot
be measured. It is reckoned only in
terms of hearts that have been lifted
up, decisions that have been changed,
men and women who, in response to
its impervious demands, have done
justice and loved kindness and
walked humbly with their God.*

—J. Carter Swaim

My son, if you accept my words
and store up my commands within you,
listening closely to wisdom
and directing your heart to understanding;
furthermore, if you call out to insight
and lift your voice to understanding,
if you seek it like silver
and search for it like hidden treasure,
then you will understand the fear of the LORD
and discover the knowledge of God.
For the LORD gives wisdom;
from His mouth come
knowledge and understanding.
He stores up success for the upright;
He is a shield for those
who live with integrity
so that He may guard the paths of justice
and protect the way of His loyal followers.

Proverbs 2:1-8

Now everyone who lives on milk is inexperienced with the message about righteousness, because he is an infant. But solid food is for the mature—for those whose senses have been trained to distinguish between good and evil.

Hebrews 5:13-14

This also comes from the LORD of Hosts.
 He gives wonderful advice;
 He gives great wisdom.

Isaiah 28:29

He gives wisdom to the wise and knowledge
 to those who have understanding.
He reveals the deep and hidden things;
 He knows what is in the darkness,
 and light dwells with Him.
I offer thanks and praise to You,
 God of my fathers, because You
 have given me wisdom and power.
And now You have let me know
 what we asked of You.

Daniel 2:21b-23a

MONEY

Instruct those who are rich in the present age not to be arrogant or to set their hope on the uncertainty of wealth, but on God, who richly provides us with all things to enjoy. Instruct them to do good, to be rich in good works, to be generous, willing to share, storing up for themselves a good foundation for the age to come.

1 Timothy 6:17-19

A CHECK ON YOUR MONEY

Some people think the only thing the Bible teaches about money is that we're supposed to give it away.

And boy, is it ever full of commands and encouragements for us to do just that! There's no doubt about it, one of the most godly, biblical, spiritual uses of money is to let it sail right through our hands and checkbooks and into the lives of other people—like into the canned food drive they're advertising in the paper, into the collection for a needy coworker's family, into the offering plate at church.

But that's not *all* God directs us to do with our money—just giving it away. In fact, giving is just one of the subsets of activity that lives under the well-known doctrine that "God owns everything." He's not only in charge of the money we earmark for church and charities, not only the ten percent (or tithe) the Bible commands us to bring to the Lord's house. He's in charge of all one hundred percent.

You probably already knew that.

But right up there with this A-one biblical concept that "God owns everything"—as in "the cattle on a thousand hills" (Psalm 50:10)—is another bit of financial theology that's equally important: our money has been given to us to invest in noble, eternal purposes.

The opposite of this principle is revealed in living color through Jesus' parable of the rich fool (Luke 12:13–21). This man's "bigger barns" approach to his money came back to haunt him one night when his life came up for account—and all he had to show for his time here on earth were goods that didn't trade in eternity's new market economy.

But "that's how it is with the one who stores up treasure for himself and is not rich toward God" (12:21).

His problem wasn't only that he hadn't been more generous, but that he hadn't put his money into something that really mattered.

So when we sink God's money into violin lessons for our daughter, we're not making a tax-deductible donation, but *we are* investing in an eternal commodity—the lives of our children and the ability for them to craft a God-given talent into a vehicle of blessing and glory they can share with others.

When we buy a tape series on learning to speak Spanish so we can at least begin to communicate with our new Hispanic neighbor, we're not writing a check to charity, but *we are* laying the foundation for a new relationship that could lead to an open door for sharing our Savior's love.

When we use our new pick-up to haul downed tree limbs from an elderly church member's yard, we're not helping build an orphanage in Haiti but *we are* helping to build up a senior saint who really needed us today.

There is nothing more eternal around you than the people you share your life with. Are you investing yourself and your money into them?

One who loves money is never satisfied with money, and whoever loves wealth is never satisfied with his income.

Ecclesiastes 5:10a

For we brought nothing into the world, and we can take nothing out. But if we have food and clothing, we will be content with these.

But those who want to be rich fall into temptation, a trap, and many foolish and harmful desires, which plunge people into ruin and destruction. For the love of money is a root of all kinds of evil, and by craving it, some have wandered away from the faith and pierced themselves with many pains.

1 Timothy 6:7-10

Your life should be free from the love of money. Be satisfied with what you have.

Hebrews 13:5a

A faithful man will have many blessings.

Proverbs 28:20a

Honor the LORD with your possessions and
    with the first produce of your entire harvest;
then your barns will be completely filled,
    and your vats will overflow with new wine.

Proverbs 3:9-10

"Bring all the tithe to the treasure house so
it may be food in My house. Prove Me in this
matter," says the LORD of Hosts. "See if I will
not open for you the gates of heaven. I will pour
out blessing for you until there is no more room
for it, and I will rebuke for you the devourer
so that it does not ruin the fruit of the ground
and that the vine in the field will not fail to
bear for you. Then all the nations will declare
you as fortunate, for you will be a land of joy."

Malachi 3:10-12

Give, and it will be given to you; a good
measure, pressed down, shaken together, and
running over will be poured into your lap.
For with the measure that you use, it will
be measured back to you.

Luke 6:38

Remember this: the person who sows sparingly will also reap sparingly, and the person who sows generously will also reap generously. Each person should do as he has decided in his heart—not out of regret or out of necessity, for God loves a cheerful giver. And God is able to make every grace overflow to you, so that in every way, always having everything you need, you may excel in every good work.

2 Corinthians 9:6-8

Most people are bothered by those passages in Scripture which they cannot understand; but as for me, I always noticed that the passages in Scripture which trouble me most are those which I do understand.

—Mark Twain

Don't collect for yourselves treasures on earth, where moth and rust destroy and where thieves break in and steal.

But collect for yourselves treasures in heaven, where neither moth nor rust destroys and where thieves don't break in and steal. For where your treasure is, there your heart will be also.

The eye is the lamp of the body. If your eye is generous, your whole body will be full of light. But if your eye is stingy, your whole body will be full of darkness. So if the light within you is darkness—how deep is that darkness!

No one can be a slave of two masters, since either he will hate one and love the other, or be devoted to one and despise the other. You cannot be slaves of God and of money.

Matthew 6:19-24

Pay your obligations to everyone: taxes to those you owe taxes, tolls to those you owe tolls, respect to those you owe respect, and honor to those you owe honor.

Romans 13:7

Better a poor man who lives with integrity than a rich man who distorts right and wrong.

Proverbs 28:6

Why does a fool have money in his hand with no intention of buying wisdom?

Proverbs 17:16

A good name is to be chosen over great wealth; favor is better than silver and gold.

Proverbs 22:1

Don't work for the food that perishes but for the food that lasts for eternal life, which the Son of Man will give you, because on Him God the Father has set His seal of approval.

John 6:27

WORTH

The first man was from the earth and made of dust; the second man is from heaven. Like the man made of dust, so are those who are made of dust; like the heavenly man, so are those who are heavenly. And just as we have borne the image of the man made of dust, we will also bear the image of the heavenly man.

1 Corinthians 15:47-49

LIKE
NEW

If there's one word to describe what we become as Christians, when God pours his purity and forgiveness into our hearts, when the Holy Spirit comes to live inside of us and rescue us from our own human nature, this is probably it:

"New."

This idea starts showing up back in the Old Testament, with the "new song" God is said to put in our mouths (Psalm 40:3) and the "something new" he is planning with the coming Messiah (Isaiah 43:19). When this Redeemer appears, the prophets tell us we are to be "called by a new name," (Isaiah 62:2), and are to be given a "new heart" and a "new spirit" to replace the ones grown hard and heavy by the corrosive effects of sin (Ezekiel 36:26).

By the time of the New Testament and the arrival of Jesus Christ into human history, all this talk about newness has become a living, breathing answer to prayer. Suddenly and with shocking force, those trying to use old ways to manipulate themselves into God's good graces are exposed as imposters. New things are everywhere in the language of Jesus and the early church founders—new "wineskins," a new "covenant," new "life," a new "way."

And still today, every time someone is captured by God's amazing grace and adopted into his forever family, this person becomes a "new man" (Ephesians 4:24), a "new creation; old things have passed away, and look, new things have come" (2 Corinthians 5:17).

Still, you may not feel all that squeaky clean today. Maybe you're in the middle of a long, failing bout with a particular sin that's had your number for much of your life. Maybe you're in one of those periods when it takes real effort to get up and go to church on Sunday morning. Maybe each time you open your Bible lately, you find it to be (in the words of the great John Bunyan, 17th-century author of *The Pilgrim's Progress*) "dry as a stick." Hey, it happens!

But try as we might, we'll never find a verse of Scripture where God says, "Furthermore, those who receive my gift of grace will always feel like it's the first day of summer vacation."

Instead, he has given us something better. He has declared that we truly *are* new—whether we feel like it or not.

The summer vacation feeling—the packing-the-car feeling, the salty-snacks-in-the-middle-of-the-front-seat feeling, the I've-got-a-week-off feeling—that's a very flighty emotion. Give it seventy-two hours, and all of a sudden it's Tuesday night, Day Three of your long anticipated vacation. When you wake up tomorrow, it'll be halfway over. You can sense it slipping away, the hours burning off faster than you can soak them in.

That's how far feelings can get you.

But God has given us an everyday reality so much deeper, so much more genuine and powerful. In him we are new. In him we have ultimate worth. In him we have everything.

Think about *that* for a while, and you might find yourself feeling a lot better real soon.

Do you not recognize for yourselves that Jesus Christ is in you?

2 Corinthians 13:5b

For in Him we live and move and exist, as even some of your own poets have said, "For we are also His offspring."

Acts 17:28

Therefore if anyone is in Christ, there is a new creation; old things have passed away, and look, new things have come.

2 Corinthians 5:17

You took off your former way of life, the old man that is corrupted by deceitful desires; you are being renewed in the spirit of your minds; you put on the new man, the one created according to God's likeness in righteousness and purity of the truth.

Ephesians 4:22-24

Brothers, consider your calling: not many are wise from a human perspective, not many powerful, not many of noble birth.

Instead, God has chosen the world's foolish things to shame the wise, and God has chosen the world's weak things to shame the strong.

God has chosen the world's insignificant and despised things—the things viewed as nothing—so He might bring to nothing the things that are viewed as something, so that no one can boast in His presence.

But from Him you are in Christ Jesus, who for us became wisdom from God, as well as righteousness, sanctification, and redemption, in order that, as it is written: "The one who boasts must boast in the Lord."

1 Corinthians 1:26-31

Indeed, it was for my own welfare that I had such great bitterness; but Your love has delivered me from the Pit of destruction, for You have thrown all my sins behind Your back.

Isaiah 38:17

Who is a God like You,
  removing iniquity and forgiving transgression
  for the remnant of His inheritance?
Who does not hold on to His anger forever,
  because He delights in faithful love.
Who will again have compassion on us;
  who will vanquish our iniquities.

Micah 7:18-19a

He made the One who did not know sin to be sin for us, so that we might become the righteousness of God in Him.

2 Corinthians 5:21

All that I am, I owe to Jesus Christ, revealed to me in his divine Book, the Bible.

–David Livingstone

When I observe Your heavens,
the work of Your fingers,
the moon and the stars,
which You set in place,
what is man, that You remember him,
the son of man, that You look after him?
You made him little less than God
and crowned him with glory and honor.
You made him lord
over the works of Your hands;
You put everything under his feet:
all the sheep and oxen,
as well as animals in the wild,
birds of the sky, and fish of the sea
passing through the currents of the seas.
O LORD, our Lord,
how magnificent is Your name
throughout the earth!

Psalm 8:3-9

He has not dealt with us as our sins deserve
or repaid us according to our offenses.
For as high as the heavens are above the earth,
so great is His faithful love
toward those who fear Him.
As far as the east is from the west,
so far has He removed
our transgressions from us.

Psalm 103:10-12

How happy are those whose lawless acts are
forgiven and whose sins are covered!

Romans 4:7

Therefore, brothers, since we have boldness
to enter the sanctuary through the blood of
Jesus, by the new and living way that He has
inaugurated for us, through the curtain (that
is, His flesh); and since we have a great high
priest over the house of God, let us draw near
with a true heart in full assurance of faith, our
hearts sprinkled clean from an evil conscience
and our bodies washed in pure water.

Hebrews 10:19-22

INTEGRITY

I will pay attention to the way of integrity. When will You come to me? I will live with integrity of heart in my house. I will not set anything godless before my eyes. I hate the doing of transgression; it will not cling to me. A devious heart will be far from me; I will not be involved with evil.

Psalm 101:2-4

ALL
TOGETHER
NOW

When most of us think of the word *integrity*, we think of workplace ethics. We think of financial accountability. We think of the most respectable people we know.

Or perhaps we think of integrity's *opposite* character trait—dishonesty—and of the corporate barons who are now living with its bitter effects by doing 10-to-20 for swindling and conniving their companies into the headlines and down the tubes.

But what does *integrity* really mean? Where does the word come from?

To understand integrity, perhaps it's helpful to place it alongside the other words in its dictionary family. Words like *integers, integral* and *integrated.*

Calling up the word *integers* may transport you back to Mrs. Clark's tenth grade algebra class, but (just as a refresher here—just for Mrs. Clark) let's recall for old-time's sake that "integers" are all the whole numbers on both side of the number line, both the negatives and the positives. Oh, and also zero, Mrs. Clark always used to say.

Next word: When we think of something being "integral" to a process, or of someone being an "integral" part of the team, we mean that this particular function or fullback is essential to making the whole apparatus work.

Finally, *integrated*. We hear a lot today about "integrated systems," the union of various computer gizmos or capabilities into one central arrangement that helps each part of the office work together. (Can you tell I don't know what I'm talking about?) Or we might think of *integration*, as when boys and girls of different races were finally put together in the same school system.

In every one of these terms and their related offshoots, the main idea is unity, entirety, completeness, of everything working together just the way it's supposed to.

So now we come back to *integrity*. And in the words of King David, we hear him asking God to "teach me your way, LORD, and I will live by Your truth. Give me an undivided mind to fear Your name" (Psalm 86:11). Men of integrity have an "undivided mind" and heart. The noble ideals they challenge their employees to pursue are the same ones they pursue themselves. The humble attitude they display in public is the same one their wives and children would say they practice at home. The careful attention they use in treating their personal finances is the same quality they bring to work each day when dealing with money that belongs to somebody else.

Therefore, men who always tell the truth don't have to possess such a sharp memory, Mark Twain said. Men who routinely act from an unwavering code of ethics are able to cut out a lot of distracting options and keep their decisions a lot more simple. Men who are always who they say they are don't have to worry about appearing to be someone they're not.

No one is more content, complete, and together than the person who lives with integrity.

A man who does not control his temper
is like a city whose wall is broken down.

Proverbs 25:28

A fool gives full vent to his anger,
but a wise man holds it in check.

Proverbs 29:11

A gossip goes around revealing a secret,
but the trustworthy keeps a confidence.

Proverbs 11:13

For we are His creation—created in Christ
Jesus for good works, which God prepared
ahead of time so that we should walk in them.

Ephesians 2:10

Righteousness guards people of integrity,
but wickedness undermines the sinner.

Proverbs 13:6

Dear friends, if our hearts do not condemn us we have confidence before God, and can receive whatever we ask from Him because we keep His commands and do what is pleasing in His sight.

1 John 3:21-22

For this is what love for God is: to keep His commands. Now His commands are not a burden.

1 John 5:3

For this is God's will, your sanctification: that you abstain from sexual immorality, so that each of you knows how to possess his own vessel in sanctification and honor, not with lustful desires, like the Gentiles who don't know God.

This means one must not transgress against and defraud his brother in this matter, because the Lord is an avenger of all these offenses, as we also previously told and warned you.

For God has not called us to impurity, but to sanctification.

1 Thessalonians 4:3-7

For the one who wants to love life
and to see good days
must keep his tongue from evil
and his lips from speaking deceit,
and he must turn away
from evil and do good.
He must seek peace and pursue it,
because the eyes of the Lord
are on the righteous
and His ears are open to their request.

1 Peter 3:10-12a

*When you have read the Bible,
you will know it is the Word of God,
because you will have found it the
key to your own heart, your own
happiness, and your own duty.*

—Woodrow Wilson

Now in a large house there are not only gold and silver bowls, but also those of wood and earthenware, some for special use, some for ordinary. So if anyone purifies himself from these things, he will be a special instrument, set apart, useful to the Master, prepared for every good work.

Flee from youthful passions, and pursue righteousness, faith, love, and peace, along with those who call on the Lord from a pure heart. But reject foolish and ignorant disputes, knowing that they breed quarrels.

The Lord's slave must not quarrel, but must be gentle to everyone, able to teach, and patient, instructing his opponents with gentleness.

Perhaps God will grant them repentance to know the truth.

2 Timothy 2:20-25

Walk as children of light—for the fruit of the light results in all goodness, righteousness, and truth—discerning what is pleasing to the Lord. Don't participate in the fruitless works of darkness, but instead, expose them. For it is shameful even to mention what is done by them in secret. Everything exposed by the light is made clear, for what makes everything clear is light.

Ephesians 5:8b-14a

Therefore, God's chosen ones, holy and loved, put on heartfelt compassion, kindness, humility, gentleness, and patience, accepting one another and forgiving one another if anyone has a complaint against another. Just as the Lord has forgiven you, so also you must forgive. Above all, put on love—the perfect bond of unity.

Colossians 3:12-14

Be alert, stand firm in the faith, be brave and strong. Your every action must be done with love.

1 Corinthians 16:13-14

PURPOSE

If I walk in the thick of danger, You will preserve my life from the anger of my enemies. You will extend Your hand; Your right hand will save me. The LORD will fulfill His purpose for me. LORD, Your love is eternal; do not abandon the work of Your hands.

Psalm 138:7-8

CAN YOU TAKE JUST ONE?

Someone said to me once, "I finally realized that there were just one or two things I could do really well. And ever since then, I've quit wasting much time on the other ones."

I don't know why that statement has stuck with me for so long, except for the fact that it's probably true.

There are a few people I've come across in my life who—oh, I don't know, maybe God just decided to really show what he could do one day, and placed into these people an unusually enormous range of talents. So every now and then, you'll meet someone who can do just about anything—sing, play the piano, fix computers, work on cars, build out their garage, you name it.

But for the huge majority of us, our list of natural abilities is in the low, single digits.

And that's good—unless we simply will not be content with the few skills or areas of expertise God placed in us at birth and expects us to multiply across a lifetime.

You think back to the parable of the talents, which Jesus told (Matthew 25). The master in this story had given a portion of money to three of his servants. To some he gave more than others—that's the master's prerogative. Two of the servants recognized that what they had been given was start-up capital, seed money. By applying their handful of talents into the 24-hour time slots we call "everyday life," they not only maximized their initial outlay but even discovered ways to grow their talents and combine them into invigorating, new areas of opportunity.

It was the guy with the one talent, though, who received the reprimand—not because he only had one talent. That would have been cruel of the master, who was the sole reason why the man had just one talent to begin with.

You know the story: The man had buried his talent. He had done nothing to enlarge and enhance it. He had not seen his gift as a treasure to be invested and returned to his master fully matured, but as a waste of time not really worth pursuing.

Surely he hadn't spent the whole period of his master's absence tending his little hole in the ground. More than likely he had tried to find something more exciting than the dim prospects he could foresee for his one little talent, something that required less effort and imagination. But wonder what kind of purpose he discovered in life, what kind of payoff he was hoping to achieve while failing to be faithful with the one thing he could really do something with?

All we really know is that his master expected the man to show simple interest in what he had been given. And that the master was dead-level serious about having his investment put into practice and acted upon.

So now we draw out our one talent, if that's what we've been given. Two, if the Lord wills. Perhaps even more, if he's chosen to ask that much of us. And we think on our life's purpose, our mission, our reason for being here.

And we ask ourselves: What will the Master say when we bring him our return?

Make your own attitude that of Christ Jesus,
    who, existing in the form of God,
    did not consider equality with God
    as something to be used
    for His own advantage.
Instead He emptied Himself
    by assuming the form of a slave,
    taking on the likeness of men.
And when He had come as a man
    in His external form, He humbled Himself
    by becoming obedient to the point
    of death—even to death on a cross.
For this reason God also highly exalted Him
    and gave Him the name that is above
    every name, so that at the name of Jesus
    every knee should bow—of those who are
    in heaven and on earth and under the
    earth—and every tongue should confess
    that Jesus Christ is Lord, to the
    glory of God the Father.

Philippians 2:5-11

For me, living is Christ.

Philippians 1:21a

Dear friends, when the fiery ordeal arises among you to test you, don't be surprised by it, as if something unusual were happening to you.

Instead, as you share in the sufferings of the Messiah rejoice, so that you may also rejoice with great joy at the revelation of His glory.

If you are ridiculed for the name of Christ, you are blessed, because the Spirit of glory and of God rests on you.

1 Peter 4:12-14

In fact, all those who want to live a godly life in Christ Jesus will be persecuted.

2 Timothy 3:12

So don't be ashamed of the testimony about our Lord. . . . Instead, share in suffering for the gospel, relying on the power of God, who has saved us and called us with a holy calling, not according to our works, but according to His own purpose and grace, which was given to us in Christ Jesus before time began.

2 Timothy 1:8-9

We know that all things work together for the good of those who love God: those who are called according to His purpose.

Romans 8:28

Many plans are in a man's heart, but the LORD's decree will prevail.

Proverbs 19:21

The Bible is to us what the star was to the wise men. But if we spend all our time in gazing upon it, observing its motions, and admiring its splendor without being led to Christ by it, the use of it will be lost to us.

—Thomas Adams

Get wisdom, get understanding;
  don't forget or turn away
  from the words of my mouth.
Don't abandon wisdom,
  and she will watch over you;
  love her, and she will guard you.
Wisdom is supreme—so get wisdom.
  And whatever else you get,
  get understanding.
Cherish her, and she will exalt you;
  if you embrace her,
  she will honor you.
She will place a garland
  of grace on your head;
  she will give you a crown of beauty. . . .
When you walk,
  your steps will not be hindered;
  when you run, you will not stumble.

Proverbs 4:5-9, 12

For this reason also, since the day we heard
this, we haven't stopped praying for you.

We are asking that you may be filled with
the knowledge of His will in all wisdom and
spiritual understanding, so that you may walk
worthy of the Lord, fully pleasing to Him,
bearing fruit in every good work and growing
in the knowledge of God. May you be strengthened with all power, according to His glorious
might, for all endurance and patience, with joy
giving thanks to the Father, who has enabled
you to share in the saints' inheritance in the
light.

Colossians 1:9-12

And in view of this, we always pray for you
that our God will consider you worthy of His
calling, and will—by His power—fulfill every
desire for goodness and the work of faith, so
that the name of our Lord Jesus will be glorified by you, and you by Him, according to the
grace of our God and the Lord Jesus Christ.

2 Thessalonians 1:11-12

DIRECTION

For I know the plans
I have for you," says the
LORD, "wholesome plans
and not harmful, to give
you a future and hope.
You will call to Me and
come and pray to Me.
Then I will listen to you.
You will seek Me and find
Me if you seek for Me
with all your heart."

Jeremiah 29:11-13

MAN
WITH A
PLAN

Never have we had so many opportunities to waste our time.

In years and generations past, when man's daily bread had to plowed, planted, and pulled from the ground, the alternatives to hard work—begging or starving—were so offensive to the human constitution, men toiled from sunup to sundown to provide for their families. They worked "from can to can't" and plopped into bed at night too tired to get into much trouble.

With the rise of the industrial and suburban age came less dependence on the farm and field, yet the God-fearing ethics inherited from parents and grandparents created an environment for widespread maturity and responsibility. And because the fun of the forties and fifties was still mostly homemade—not on sale at the store—people tended to work and live and behave like they should.

Today, we're in the middle of an odd tension. On one hand, the wildly competitive nature of the modern job market has most of us scrambling to keep up. Work is lean and mean and long and hard. It nests in the back of our minds at night and over the weekend, challenging us to think smarter, be more creative, and catch the earliest wave before the others can catch up.

Yet on the other hand, our consumer-crazed society has multiplied the ways we can spend whatever free time is left over.

Movies—twenty-seven screens at one theater.

Television—with a channel for every taste and temptation.

DVDs—now with trailers and trivia games to go along with their two-hour films.

Internet—more sports scores and stock reports than we can possibly digest.

Shopping—something for someone on every street corner.

So on top of the work that consumes us already, we're constantly being asked:

• "Have you seen this?"

- "Have you been there?"
- "Have you heard about . . . ?"
- "Have you checked this out?

In chasing all these options and opportunities—in trying to make sure we're culturally competent and amply entertained—many of our lives have become non-stop examples of activity. We're here, we're there, we're everywhere.

But are we where we hoped to be?

Are we where we meant to be going?

Are we moving but not getting anywhere?

Many of us today are in need of a plan. Not just any old plan. Not a plan to be a millionaire or to make ourselves comfortable. We need God's plan for our lives. We need to wake up each day knowing that the things most important to him are the things most important to us—the things we're not willing to wait till retirement to do something about, but itching to put into practice today.

How are you coming on *that* plan? And how will it change your plans for this weekend?

Commit your activities to the LORD
and your plans will be achieved.

Proverbs 16:3

Plans fail when there is no counsel,
but with many advisers they succeed.

Proverbs 15:22

The counsel of the LORD stands forever,
the plans of His heart
from generation to generation.

Psalm 33:11

I know You can do anything;
no plan of Yours can be denied.

Job 42:2

May He give you what your heart desires
and fulfill your whole purpose.

Psalm 20:4

What the wicked dreads
will come upon him,
but what the righteous desires
will be given to him.

Proverbs 10:24

Not that I have already reached the goal or
am already fully mature, but I make every
effort to take hold of it because I also have
been taken hold of by Christ Jesus.

Brothers, I do not consider myself to have
taken hold of it. But one thing I do: forgetting
what is behind and reaching forward to what is
ahead, I pursue as my goal the prize promised
by God's heavenly call in Christ Jesus.

Philippians 3:12-14

For we know that if our earthly house, a
tent, is destroyed, we have a building from
God, a house not made with hands, eternal in
the heavens. . . . And the One who prepared us
for this very thing is God, who gave us the
Spirit as a down payment.

2 Corinthians 5:1, 5

Though we are always confident and know that while we are at home in the body we are away from the Lord—for we walk by faith, not by sight—yet we are confident and satisfied to be out of the body and at home with the Lord. Therefore, whether we are at home or away, we make it our aim to be pleasing to Him.

2 Corinthians 5:6-9

For we are convinced that we have a clear conscience, wanting to conduct ourselves honorably in everything.

Hebrews 13:18b

The Word of God will stand a thousand readings. And he who has gone over it most frequently is the surest of finding new wonders there.

—James Hamilton

Commit your way to the LORD;
   trust in Him, and He will act,
   making your righteousness
   shine like the dawn,
   your justice like the noonday.
Be silent before the LORD
   and wait expectantly for Him;
   do not be agitated by one
   who prospers in his way,
   by the man who carries out evil plans.
Refrain from anger and give up your rage;
   do not be agitated—
   it can only bring harm.
For evildoers will be destroyed,
   but those who hope in the LORD
   will inherit the land.

Psalm 37:5-9

The LORD makes poor and gives wealth;
  He humbles and He exalts.
He raises the poor from the dust
  and lifts the needy from the ash heap.
He seats them with noblemen
  and grants them a throne of honor.
For the foundations of the earth
  belong to the LORD;
  He has set the world on them.
He guards the feet of His devout followers,
  but the wicked are silenced in the darkness
  for it is not through strength
  that a man prevails.

1 Samuel 2:7-9

I am able to do all things through Him who
strengthens me.

Philippians 4:13

No wisdom, no understanding,
  and no counsel will prevail against the LORD.
A horse is prepared for the day of battle,
  but victory comes from the LORD.

Proverbs 21:30-31

SCRIPTURE

I will meditate on Your precepts and think about Your ways. I will delight in Your statutes; I will not forget Your word. . . . Your statutes are the theme of my song during my earthly life. I remember Your name in the night, LORD, and I keep Your law. This is my practice: I obey Your precepts.

Psalm 119:15-16, 54-56

Nothing But The Truth

The truth is.

And it's in the Bible.

That's why if we want to survive, we can't help but be in there ourselves.

I mean, they don't always tell the truth on *60 Minutes*. Or in the editorial pages of the daily newspaper. Or around the lunch table at work.

But you can start each day with healthy doses of truth, right beside your toast and jelly, right in the middle of your getting-ready routine, perhaps even right before you peel out of bed and put your feet on the floor.

And who knows what you'll find inside there?

You may come across a section of Scripture that speaks so clearly to a situation you're facing in your family, you wonder what the chances are that you'd be reading this particular passage today. You look away from the page and lift your chin a couple of inches, whispering into the air, "Thank you, Lord, for showing me this." Wow.

You may find yourself in a storyline you've known since you were a kid, but you never noticed, for example, that after Daniel had been lifted unharmed out of the lion's den and they tossed in his accusers, their bodies didn't even hit the floor before the lions had torn them apart. Cool.

You may find a verse you'd underlined years ago and your eye is drawn back to it again. Perhaps it's Psalm 115:1: "Not to us, LORD, not to us, but to Your name give glory because of Your faithful love, because of Your truth." You're reminded again that whatever you may be given credit for today, the honor really goes to God, who gave you every blessing and ability you have. Right?

You may stumble across a verse that's hard to understand. Like when Jesus told his disciples, just before he fed the five thousand: "You give them something to eat" (Luke 9:13). What did he expect them to do? Take everybody's orders for pizza and see if they could find a place that delivered? Jesus knew, of course, that these twelve men couldn't pull fish and chips out of mid-air, so why would he say that? The light starts to come on: Maybe he wanted them to learn this lesson—to never look first to their own strengths and abilities—to always think this line before jumping to conclusions: "I'll bet Jesus can do something about this!" Yeah.

Or maybe an answer doesn't come right away. Maybe you're still not sure, even after thinking about it for a good, long while, why it would be important for us to know how many sheep, cattle, and donkeys were taken in plunder from the Midianites (Numbers 31). Why so specific? Why is this on the same Bible paper as John 3:16? Who cares? Hmm.

But even wrestling with truth is better than being ignorant of it. You just never know what spiritual adventure and direction awaits you between the covers of your Bible. But you do know this: whatever you read there will be more true than anything else you hear all day.

Every word of God is pure;
   He is a shield to those
   who take refuge in Him.

Proverbs 30:5

How happy are those whose way is blame-
less,
   who live according to the law of the LORD!
Happy are those who keep His decrees
   and seek Him with all their heart.

Psalm 119:1-2

For whatever was written before was
written for our instruction, so that through
our endurance and through the encouragement
of the Scriptures we may have hope.

Romans 15:4

Remember Your word to Your servant,
   through which You have given me hope.
This is my comfort in my affliction:
   Your promise has given me life.

Psalm 119:49-50

As for you, continue in what you have learned and firmly believed, knowing those from whom you learned, and that from childhood you have known the sacred Scriptures, which are able to instruct you for salvation through faith in Christ Jesus.

2 Timothy 3:14-15

The wise will be put to shame;
  they will be dismayed and snared.
They have rejected the word of the LORD,
  so what wisdom do they really have?

Jeremiah 8:9

I have Your decrees as a heritage forever;
  indeed, they are the joy of my heart.
I am resolved to obey Your statutes
  to the very end.

Psalm 119:111-112

Your word is completely pure,
  and Your servant loves it.

Psalm 119:140

Lᴏʀᴅ, Your word is forever;
  it is firmly fixed in heaven. . . .
They stand today in accordance with Your
  judgments, for all things are Your servants.
If Your instruction had not been my delight,
  I would have died in my affliction.
I will never forget Your precepts,
  for You have given me life through them. . . .
I have seen a limit to all perfection,
  but Your command is without limit.

Psalm 119:89, 91-93, 96

*God himself has condescended to
teach the way. For this very end he
came from heaven. And he hath
written it down in a book. O give
me that Book! At any price, give
me the Book of God!*

—John Wesley

The instruction of the LORD
is perfect, reviving the soul;
the testimony of the LORD is trustworthy,
making the inexperienced wise.
The precepts of the LORD are right,
making the heart glad;
the commandment of the LORD is radiant,
making the eyes light up.
The fear of the LORD is pure, enduring forever;
the ordinances of the LORD
are reliable and altogether righteous.
They are more desirable than gold—
than an abundance of pure gold;
and sweeter than honey—
than honey dripping from the comb.
In addition, Your servant is warned by them;
there is great reward in keeping them.

Psalm 19:7-11

I delight to do Your will, my God;
Your instruction resides within me.

Psalm 40:8

Your decrees are my delight
and my counselors.

Psalm 119:24

I rejoice in the way revealed by Your decrees
as much as in all riches.

Psalm 119:14

Long ago I learned from Your decrees
that You have established them forever.

Psalm 119:152

The entirety of Your word is truth,
and all Your righteous judgments
endure forever.

Psalm 119:160

WORSHIP

Better a day in Your courts than a thousand anywhere else. I would rather be at the door of the house of my God than to live in the tents of the wicked. For the LORD God is a sun and shield. The LORD gives grace and glory; He does not withhold the good from those who live with integrity.

Psalm 84:10-11

SOUND CHECK

You may be one of those people for whom worship comes easily. You may catch yourself whistling a praise tune while painting or at the post office. You may have no problem losing yourself in a church service, lifting your hands and closing your eyes, freely expressing what you feel in your heart.

That's good.

Or you may be one of those people who just don't go in for all of that. You love the Lord. You're every bit as much a believer as they are. But your worship is more of an internal, reflective response. You're not as likely to respond to a compliment with "praise the Lord" as you are with a sincere "thank you."

And that's good too.

But here's what's bad.

Some of you who find worship a natural reflex look down on those brothers who don't feel as free with their hands and feet as you do. You can't understand how a person could have a genuine relationship with Christ and not be fogging up their glasses with their radiant tears. I mean, we ought to be able to see some spirituality.

But others of you think your fellow Christians who clap and sway and don't sing with the songbooks are flirting with God's wrath. At the least it's a distraction, and at the worst it's downright irreverent. And those who can't go to church without showing God some respect might be better off not going at all.

Well, let's put this straight.

Most of you who love your worship loud and lively are reflecting the temperament God gave you. It's the way you feel most comfortable expressing your praise, and it comes from a place inside of you that's bubbling over with love for Jesus. But you have to be careful: It's easy to let this kind of worship style slip over into mere emotion. If you're not sure the Holy Spirit can show up without a drum set and a chord change, you are most likely watching your worship take on just as much of a form and routine as you despise in other settings.

Likewise, the more calm and traditional ones of you are generally gravitating toward your personality type. You have no need to feel inferior or less enthusiastic about your faith just because you prefer worship services that are more serene and subdued. But you must be on your guard against the going-through-the-motions, doing-it-in-your-sleep temptations that are the stock-in-trade of the devil. He loves to see your worship reduced to habit and rote, the kind you whip through without thinking.

Worship styles can flip-flop and fluctuate over time. What's in and what's out can become points of Christian contention.

But we'll do each other and our combined witness a great, big favor by appreciating and enjoying what God is doing in each sector and segment of his body.

There's truly enough love to go around.

Come, let us worship and bow down;
   let us kneel before the LORD our Maker.
For He is our God, and we are the people
   of His pasture, the sheep under His care.

Psalm 95:6-7

We all went astray like sheep;
   we all have turned to our own way.
   and the LORD has punished Him
   for the iniquity of all of us.

Isaiah 53:6

For you know the grace of our Lord Jesus
Christ: although He was rich, for your sake He
became poor, so that by His poverty you might
become rich.

2 Corinthians 8:9

My salvation and glory depend on God;
   my strong rock, my refuge, is in God.
Trust in Him at all times, you people;
   pour out your hearts before Him.
God is our refuge.

Psalm 62:7-8

Whom do I have in heaven but You?
And I desire nothing on earth but You.
My flesh and my heart may fail,
but God is the strength of my heart,
my portion forever.

Psalm 73:25-26

God—His way is perfect;
the word of the LORD is pure.
He is a shield to all
who take refuge in Him.
For who is God besides the LORD?
And who is a rock? Only our God.
God—He clothes me with strength
and makes my way perfect.
He makes my feet like the feet of a deer
and sets me securely on the heights.

Psalm 18:30-33

Clap your hands, all you peoples;
shout to God with a jubilant cry.
For the LORD Most High is awe-inspiring,
a great King over all the earth.

Psalm 47:1-2

Shout triumphantly to the LORD, all the earth.
  Serve the LORD with gladness;
  come before Him with joyful songs.
Acknowledge that the LORD is God.
  He made us, and we are His—
  His people, the sheep of His pasture.
Enter His gates with thanksgiving
  and His courts with praise.
Give thanks to Him and praise His name.
  For the LORD is good, and His love is eternal;
  His faithfulness endures
  through all generations.

Psalm 100:1-5

*The Bible furnishes the only fitting
vehicle to express the thoughts that
overwhelm us when contemplating
the stellar universe.*

—O. M. Mitchell

Ascribe to the LORD,
   O families of the peoples,
   ascribe to the LORD glory and strength.
Ascribe to the LORD the glory due His name;
   bring an offering and come before Him.
Worship the LORD in His holy majesty;
   tremble before Him, all the earth.
The world is firmly established;
   it cannot be shaken.
Let the heavens be glad and the earth rejoice,
   and let them say among the nations,
   "The LORD is King!"
Let the sea and everything in it resound;
   let the fields and all that is in them exult.
Then the trees of the forest
   will shout for joy before the LORD,
   for He comes to judge the earth.

1 Chronicles 16:28-33

Oh, the depth of the riches
both of the wisdom
and the knowledge of God!
How unsearchable His judgments
and untraceable His ways!
For who has known the mind of the Lord?
Or who has been His counselor?
Or who has ever first given to Him,
and has to be repaid?
For from Him and through Him
and to Him are all things.

Romans 11:33-36a

Let the message about the Messiah dwell
richly among you, teaching and admonishing
one another in all wisdom, and singing psalms,
hymns, and spiritual songs, with gratitude in
your hearts to God.

Colossians 3:16

May the LORD, the God of Israel,
be praised from everlasting to everlasting.

1 Chronicles 16:36

PRAYER

Asa cried out to the LORD his God: "O LORD, there is no difference for You whether You help the mighty or those without strength. Help us, O LORD our God, for we depend on You, and in Your name we have come against this multitude. O LORD, You are our God. Do not let a mere mortal hinder You."

2 Chronicles 14:11

You Talking to Me?

Chuck Swindoll tells of a time when he was driving through town one day, praying aloud in his car at an intersection. When he caught out of the corner of his eye a next-door driver who was starting to stare, Swindoll spooled down his window and playfully shouted, "I'm not talking to you!"

That's right. Then who *are* we talking to?

One of my good mentoring friends once advised me to be careful about this: to be sure that when I'm praying, I'm talking to God and not to myself.

It's a real temptation, isn't it? How often have you looked up during your prayer time and realized that you're no longer talking with God but have been carrying on a conversation with *yourself* for ten minutes. Or with the brother-in-law who's not being very husbandly to your kid sister. Or with the boss who's been making your work harder than it already is.

We tend to get distracted in prayer—our lives and minds so full of issues, concerns, and problems that sticking to one subject for very long is a real exercise. But the discipline of staying attentive during prayer is a *must* if we want to experience all the things prayer is supposed to be about. It doesn't take some kind of weird focusing technique, simply a heartfelt desire to be with God, to want his ear, to know that we need him.

For maybe that's what the main problem is anyway: we're not sure we need him. We pray because we're supposed to. We pray because we know he expects it of us. But even in the middle of our prayer, we're off fixing our problems our own way, dealing with our frustrations by ourselves, forming logical arguments for the plan of action we're considering.

Try this: even if you wake up in the morning mad at yourself for being unkind to your wife the night before, even if you've been tossing and turning with a decision to make at the office, even if you've been nursing a nagging pain in your side that's possibly more than simple soreness, just set everything else to one side for a moment—your guilt, sadness, worry, stress, whatever—and concentrate on Jesus.

See him the way John saw him while writing his Revelation: "His head and hair were white like wool—white as snow, His eyes like a fiery flame, His feet were like bronze fired in a furnace, and His voice like the sound of cascading waters. In His right hand He had seven stars; from His mouth came a sharp two-edged sword; and His face was shining like the sun at midday" (Revelation 1:14–16).

When John saw this sight—the resurrected, glorified radiance of the One who had been his beloved friend on earth—*even he* "fell at His feet like a dead man." But Jesus "laid His right hand on me, and said, 'Don't be afraid! I am the First and the Last, and the Living One. I was dead, but look—I am alive forever and ever'" (1:17–18).

We may think we can handle our daily difficulties by talking things over with ourselves. But we have a Savior who is more than able to give us direction, and more than willing to put his arm around us and take us there.

If we'll give him our undivided attention.

Let me experience Your faithful love
  in the morning, for I trust in You.
Reveal to me the way I should go,
  because I long for You.
Rescue me from my enemies, LORD;
  I come to You for protection.
Teach me to do Your will,
  for You are my God.
May Your gracious Spirit
  lead me on level ground.

Psalm 143:8-10

Now this is the confidence we have before
Him: whenever we ask anything according to
His will, He hears us. And if we know that He
hears whatever we ask, we know that we have
what we have asked Him for.

1 John 5:14-15

Keep asking, and it will be given to you.
Keep searching, and you will find. Keep
knocking, and the door will be opened to you.

Matthew 7:7

I cry aloud to God,
   aloud to God, and He will hear me.
                              Psalm 77:1

The LORD is near all who call out to Him,
   all who call out to Him with integrity.
He fulfills the desires of those who fear Him;
   He hears their cry for help and saves them.
                              Psalm 145:18-19

You will petition Him,
   and He will hear you. . . .
Light will shine on your ways.
                              Job 22:27a, 28b

Be gracious to me, Lord,
   for I call to You all day long.
Bring joy to Your servant's life,
   since I set my hope on You, Lord.
For You, Lord, are kind and ready to forgive,
   abundant in faithful love
   to all who call on You.
                              Psalm 86:3-5

O God, You are my God;
  I eagerly seek You.
My soul thirsts for You;
  my body faints for You in a land
  that is dry, desolate, and without water.
So I gaze on You in the sanctuary
  to see Your strength and Your glory.
My lips will glorify You
  because Your faithful love is better than life.
So I will praise You as long as I live;
  at Your name, I will lift up my hands.
You satisfy me as with rich food;
  my mouth will praise You with joyful lips.

Psalm 63:1-5

*I know the Bible is inspired because
it finds me at greater depths of my
being than any other book.*
  —Samuel Taylor Coleridge

Come and see the works of God;
　His acts toward mankind
　are awe-inspiring. . . .
Come and listen, all who fear God,
　and I will tell what He has done for me.
I cried out to Him with my mouth,
　and praise was on my tongue.
If I had been aware of malice in my heart,
　the Lord would not have listened.
However, God has listened;
　He has paid attention
　to the sound of my prayer.
May God be praised!
　He has not turned away my prayer
　or turned His faithful love from me.

Psalm 66:5, 16-20

Call on Me in a day of trouble;
  I will rescue you, and you will honor Me.

Psalm 50:15

Even before they call, I will answer;
  while they are still speaking, I will hear.

Isaiah 65:24

How happy is the man
  who has put his trust in the LORD
  and has not turned to the proud
  or to those who run after lies!
LORD my God, You have done many things—
  Your wonderful works and Your plans for us;
  none can compare with You.
If I were to report and speak of them,
  they are more than can be told.

Psalm 40:4-5

But as for me, I will watch for the LORD;
  I will wait for the God who saves me.
My God will hear me.

Micah 7:7

SERVICE

Now finally, all of you should be like-minded and sympathetic, should love believers, and be compassionate and humble, not paying back evil for evil or insult for insult but, on the contrary, giving a blessing, since you were called for this, so that you can inherit a blessing.

1 Peter 3:8-9

THE SERVANT'S STORY

If you find yourself in Luke 17 anytime soon, you'll come across a little parable that doesn't usually make it into the children's Bible story books. In fact, I'd hazard a guess that a whole of lot of church-going Christians have never heard of it. I know I surely didn't notice it until recently.

This is a chapter that features some famous texts. You've got the "better a millstone around your neck" warning for those who cause children to stumble or to question God. You've got the story about the one healed leper out of ten who came back to say thanks to Jesus. You've got the vivid end-time imagery of two people side-by-side—one is taken; one is left. Good stuff.

But tucked away in verses 7–10 is the parable of a slave who's put in a hard day's work—plowing the fields, tending the sheep. He comes in wringing with sweat, tired and hungry. His master calls to him from the table, "Hey, Joe! Come sit down and have some dinner with me."

Uh . . . not exactly.

Instead the master greets him at the door and says to his worn-out slave: "So, what's for supper?" Later on, of course, this main man of the house will be glad for his servant to refresh himself, but for now there's a master who needs serving. There's everything that's needed for preparing a meal in the kitchen. There's a duty to perform. So the slave washes his hands and face and starts whipping up some grub.

Now, who's the bad guy in this story? The slave-driving master? Our sensitive modern ears tell us so. We'd like to think the master would understand how tired and sore his servant is. We'd be impressed if he'd tie the apron around his own paunchy waist and get enough for the two of them. But for all we know, the master doesn't even "thank that slave because he did what he was commanded" (verse 9). I mean, how rude and inhuman can you get!

But Jesus sums up the story with these surprising words. "In the same way, when you have done all that you were commanded, you should say, 'We are good-for-nothing slaves; we've only done our duty' " (verse 10).

This may sound hard on the self-esteem. This may not seem to wash with our picture of a foot-washing Savior. This slavery business strikes us below the belt. There must be some other way of interpreting this passage.

But verse 10 is for us. We are the servants of the living God. We may get tired and hungry and disgruntled and out of sorts. But we must never get to the point where he could make a demand of us and we would rear up our backs in defiance.

It is not the opposite of love to expect obedience. But it is the opposite of love for us to withhold obedience.

We know that in God's eyes we are not "good-for-nothing." If so, then why would he have paid such a high price for our souls? But we must be careful that in celebrating our value we do not demean his. We have a duty to perform. And we can never give back more than we've been given.

Everything is permissible," but not everything builds up. No one should seek his own good, but the good of the other person.

1 Corinthians 10:23b-24

If a brother or sister is without clothes and lacks daily food, and one of you says to them, "Go in peace, keep warm, and eat well," but you don't give them what the body needs, what good is it?

James 2:15-16

But when you give to the poor, don't let your left hand know what your right hand is doing, so that your giving may be in secret. And your Father who sees in secret will reward you.

Matthew 6:3-4

Therefore, through Him let us continually offer up to God a sacrifice of praise, that is, the fruit of our lips that confess His name. Don't neglect to do good and to share, for God is pleased with such sacrifices.

Hebrews 13:15-16

Render true justice; show faithful love and compassion to one another. Do not oppress the widow or the orphan, the stranger, or the poor, and do not plot evil in your hearts against one another.

Zechariah 7:9b-10

All bitterness, anger and wrath, insult and slander must be removed from you, along with all wickedness. And be kind and compassionate to one another, forgiving one another, just as God also forgave you in Christ.

Ephesians 4:31-32

Carry one another's burdens; in this way you will fulfill the law of Christ.

Galatians 6:2

For where envy and selfish ambition exist, there is disorder and every kind of evil. But the wisdom from above is first pure, then peace-loving, gentle, compliant, full of mercy and good fruits, without favoritism and hypocrisy.

James 3:16-17

The one who despises his neighbor sins,
but whoever shows kindness
to the poor will be happy.

Proverbs 14:21

The one who oppresses the poor
insults their Maker, but one who
is kind to the needy honors Him.

Proverbs 14:31

A generous person will be enriched,
and the one who gives a drink
of water will receive water.

Proverbs 11:25

*I read my Bible to know what people
ought to be doing, and my newspaper
to know what they are doing.*
—John Henry Newman

Is this not the fast that I would choose:
  To break the chains of wickedness,
  to untie the ropes of the yoke,
  to set the oppressed free,
  and to tear off every yoke?
Is it not to share your bread with the hungry,
  to bring the poor and homeless one
  into your house, to clothe the naked
  when you see him, and not to turn
  your backs on your own flesh and blood?
Then your light will appear like the dawn,
  and your recovery will come quickly.
Your righteousness will go before you,
  and the LORD's glory will be your rear guard.
At that time, when you call,
  the LORD will answer;
  when you cry out,
  He will say, "Here I am."

Isaiah 58:6-9a

Do nothing out of rivalry or conceit, but in humility consider others as more important than yourselves. Everyone should look out not only for his own interests, but also for the interests of others.

Philippians 2:3-4

Since you put away lying, speak the truth, each one to his neighbor, because we are members of one another. . . . No rotten talk should come from your mouth, but only what is good for the building up of someone in need, in order to give grace to those who hear.

Ephesians 4:25, 29

Now may the God of peace, who brought up from the dead our Lord Jesus—the great Shepherd of the sheep—with the blood of the everlasting covenant, equip you with all that is good to do His will, working in us what is pleasing in His sight, through Jesus Christ, to whom be glory forever and ever.

Hebrews 13:20-21

ACCOUNTABILITY

I pray that your participation in the faith may become effective through knowing every good thing that is in us for the glory of Christ. For I have great joy and encouragement from your love, because the hearts of the saints have been refreshed through you, brother.

Philemon 6-7

ONE
FOR ALL

We need each other.

This is a fact that comes hard for some of us. It'd be nice to be self-sufficient. It would be freeing for a supervisor to tell us our performance was so superior, we no longer needed an annual evaluation. It would be a lot more convenient if we could simply diagnose and treat ourselves.

But we can't. We need work crews to pave and repair the roads we drive on. We need systems guys to keep our telecommunications zipping at high speeds. We need delivery men to make sure our mom's birthday present arrives at her house on time.

And we need Christian friends to keep our feet in the straight and narrow. This is not news to us. Even if this used to be rarely practiced in any deliberate fashion, the last several years have shown a huge spike in the number of men actively involved in accountability relationships. This is all good, and we can pray it will always continue.

But accountability groups could meet every morning, noon, and night of the week and still be little more than gripe collectors if not for the Word of God being their sole source of wisdom and truth.

A lot of us have seen some of these accountability set-ups become permission points for people to feel better about their sinful attitudes and behaviors. We've listened and laughed and been afraid to really confront, because we didn't want to sound too over-the-top. We've been pulled in by somebody's line, even though we've known that their spiritual talk wasn't really working its way down into their spirits.

Accountability that doesn't hold us very accountable is probably not worth the coffee money we spend on it. We shouldn't feel confirmed and comfortable just because our prayer partners have given us their sympathetic approval. Our ultimate accountability is always to God and his Word.

So put a tight check on the accountability relationships in your life:

• Do you mostly just spill and share without searching the Bible for answers and guidance?

• Does everybody feel free to speak up when worldliness is being passed off as Christian living?

• Are "I know the Bible says this, but . . . " statements given room to be affirmed and accepted?

• Are committed members willing to be challenged and corrected by biblical counsel?

• Is everyone proving themselves to be a serious student of God's Word themselves?

Like I said, accountability groups are great. Those of us who enjoy them will quickly attest to how helpful they've been in our own lives, and how encouraging it's been to get to know other men so well.

But we just need a little reminder every now and then—a reminder that the purpose of a men's group is to inspire us to become more like Christ. It's supposed to help us become always-on-call ambassadors of his kingdom, living the kind of life that's characterized by *difference*, not by average American living with a Bible verse on top.

And we can do it. Together.

How good and pleasant it is
  when brothers can live together! . . .
For there the LORD has appointed
  the blessing—life forevermore.

Psalm 133:1, 3b

Therefore, brothers, stand firm and hold to
the traditions you were taught, either by our
message or by our letter. May our Lord Jesus
Christ Himself and God our Father, who has
loved us and given us eternal encouragement
and good hope by grace, encourage your hearts
and strengthen you in every good work and
word.

2 Thessalonians 2:15-17

Let us hold on to the confession of our hope
without wavering, for He who promised is faithful. And let us be concerned about one another
in order to promote love and good works, not
staying away from our meetings, as some habit-
ually do, but encouraging each other, and all
the more as you see the day drawing near.

Hebrews 10:23-25

A friend loves at all times,
and a brother is born for a difficult time.

Proverbs 17:17

A man with many friends
may be harmed, but there is a friend
who stays closer than a brother.

Proverbs 18:24

I am a friend to all who fear You,
to those who keep Your precepts.

Psalm 119:63

The wounds of a friend are trustworthy.

Proverbs 27:6a

It is better to listen to rebuke from a wise person
than to listen to the song of fools.

Ecclesiastes 7:5

Teach me, and I will be silent.
Help me understand what I did wrong.

Job 6:24

The one who says he is in the light but hates his brother is in the darkness until now. The one who loves his brother remains in the light, and there is no cause for stumbling in him.

1 John 2:9-10

Anyone who ignores instruction despises himself, but whoever listens to correction acquires good sense.

Proverbs 15:32

We read the Bible to be fed. We read it to be converted, to be strengthened, to be taught, to be rebuked, to be counseled, to be comforted.

—Richard Foster

How happy is the man
 who does not follow
 the advice of the wicked,
 or take the path of sinners,
 or join a group of mockers!
Instead, his delight
 is in the LORD's instruction,
 and he meditates on it day and night.
He is like a tree planted
 beside streams of water
 that bears its fruit in season
 and whose leaf does not wither.
 Whatever he does prospers. . . .
For the LORD watches over
 the way of the righteous,
 but the way of the wicked
 leads to ruin.

Psalm 1:1-3, 6

Watch out, brothers, so that there won't be in any of you an evil, unbelieving heart that departs from the living God.

But encourage each other daily, while it is still called today, so that none of you is hardened by sin's deception. For we have become companions of the Messiah if we hold firmly until the end the reality that we had at the start.

Hebrews 3:12-14

Love must be without hypocrisy. Detest evil; cling to what is good. Show family affection to one another with brotherly love. Outdo one another in showing honor.

Romans 12:9-10

May the God of endurance and encouragement grant you agreement with one another, according to Christ Jesus, so that you may glorify the God and Father of our Lord Jesus Christ with a united mind and voice.

Therefore accept one another, just as the Messiah also accepted you, to the glory of God.

Romans 15:5-7

PASSION

Blessed be the God and Father of our Lord Jesus Christ. According to His great mercy, He has given us a new birth into a living hope through the resurrection of Jesus Christ from the dead, and into an inheritance that is imperishable, uncorrupted, and unfading, kept in heaven for you.

1 Peter 1:3-4

READY TO GO?

I'm ready, are you?

Ready to start letting *God's* will for my next twenty-four hours determine what *my* will should be.

Ready to throw off the stupid sins that have clogged my commitment to Christ for the last time.

Ready to meet my neighbors.

Ready to do my best.

Ready to turn off the television long enough to soak some quiet into this room.

Ready to say yes the first time I'm asked to serve somebody.

Ready to realize the importance of my family.

Ready to go to church Sunday morning with a heart that's been worshiping since last night.

Ready to jump into a reason bigger than myself.

Ready to live with an eternal perspective.

Ready to not feel entitled to my own comfort and luxury.

Ready to get all my approval needs met in God without needing it from anyone else.

Ready to be his when it hurts.

Ready to know more Bible verses than I do ball scores.

Ready to invest in people instead of things.

Ready to give up an old habit rather than miss a new opportunity.

Ready to pour it on and pour it out.

Ready to put a letter in the mail I've been meaning to write for a month.

Ready to take time to stop and think before I say something I shouldn't.

Ready to quit judging others and feeling like I'm so superior.

Ready to make Christ my first conscious thought of the morning and my last thought before bed.

Ready to read the paper as a way of feeding my prayer list, not my news fix.

Ready to tell someone about Jesus before the day's out.

Ready to love the things God loves, and to hate the things he despises.

Ready to let God squeeze all the selfishness out my attitudes and affections.

Ready to be available to him at any point of the day.

Ready to make sure my children know how valuable they are to me.

Ready to skip a meal in order to buy lunch for someone who may not have one otherwise.

Ready to give God full control of my financial decisions.

Ready to treat my wife with love, honor, and gratitude.

Ready to stand up for Christ no matter what it costs me.

Ready to care and share and bathe everything in prayer.

I'm ready to be who God has called me to be.

Aren't you?

Dear friends, we are God's children now,
and what we will be has not yet been revealed.
We know that when He appears, we will be
like Him, because we will see Him as He is.
And everyone who has this hope in Him purifies himself just as He is pure.

1 John 3:2-3

The hope of the righteous is joy, but the
   expectation of the wicked comes to nothing.

Proverbs 10:28

I keep the LORD in mind always.
   Because He is at my right hand,
   I will not be defeated.
Therefore my heart is glad, and my spirit
   rejoices; my body also rests securely.
For You will not abandon me to Sheol;
   You will not allow Your
   Faithful One to see the Pit.
You reveal the path of life to me;
   in Your presence is abundant joy;
   in Your right hand are eternal pleasures.

Psalm 16:8-11

If we have placed our hope in Christ for this life only, we should be pitied more than anyone.

1 Corinthians 15:19

For we too were once foolish, disobedient, deceived, captives of various passions and pleasures, living in malice and envy, hateful, detesting one another. But when the goodness and love for man appeared from God our Savior, He saved us—not by works of righteousness that we had done, but according to His mercy, through the washing of regeneration and renewal by the Holy Spirit.

Titus 3:3-5

For when you were slaves of sin, you were free from allegiance to righteousness. And what fruit was produced then from the things you are now ashamed of? For the end of those things is death.

But now, since you have been liberated from sin and become enslaved to God, you have your fruit, which results in sanctification—and the end is eternal life!

Romans 6:20-22

We have obtained access by faith into this grace in which we stand, and we rejoice in the hope of the glory of God. And not only that, but we also rejoice in our afflictions, because we know that affliction produces endurance, endurance produces proven character, and proven character produces hope. This hope does not disappoint, because God's love has been poured out in our hearts through the Holy Spirit who was given to us.

Romans 5:2b-5

The Bible is the truest utterance that ever came by alphabetic letters, through which, as through a window divinely opened, all men can look into the stillness of eternity and discern in glimpses their far-distant, long-forgotten home.
—Thomas Carlyle

Listen! I am telling you a mystery:
  We will not all fall asleep,
  but we will all be changed,
  in a moment, in the twinkling of an eye,
  at the last trumpet. . . .
Now when this corruptible
  is clothed with incorruptibility,
  and this mortal is clothed with immortality,
  then the saying that is written will take place:
  "Death has been swallowed up in victory."
O Death, where is your victory?
  O Death, where is your sting?
Now the sting of death is sin,
  and the power of sin is the law.
But thanks be to God,
  who gives us the victory
  through our Lord Jesus Christ!
                    1 Corinthians 15:51-52a, 54-57

So if you have been raised with the Messiah, seek what is above, where the Messiah is, seated at the right hand of God. Set your minds on what is above, not on what is on the earth.

For you have died, and your life is hidden with the Messiah in God. When the Messiah, who is your life, is revealed, then you also will be revealed with Him in glory.

Colossians 3:1-4

For the grace of God has appeared, with salvation for all people, instructing us to deny godlessness and worldly lusts and to live in a sensible, righteous, and godly way in the present age, while we wait for the blessed hope and the appearing of the glory of our great God and Savior, Jesus Christ.

Titus 2:11-13

Now may the God of hope fill you with all joy and peace in believing, so that you may overflow with hope by the power of the Holy Spirit.

Romans 15:13